THE FLYING SABUKI

A Father-Son Nature Adventure

E.S. CURRY

cognition
.media

The Flying Sabuki

A Father-Son Nature Adventure

By E.S. Curry

1. FAMILY & RELATIONSHIPS: Parenting - Fatherhood 2. TRAVEL: Family Travel *see* Special Interest - Family 3. SELF-HELP: Motivational & Inspirational

ISBN: 978-1-954059-00-9 (paperback)

ISBN: 978-1-954059-01-6 (ebook)

Library of Congress Control Number: 2021924287

Cover by E.S. Curry

Edited by Beth Lynn and Wendy Lindstrom

First Edition

Printed in United States of America

Cognition.Media, Shaker Heights, OH

Visit the author's website at escurry.com

This book is typeset in Hoefler.

For Åsmund

PREFACE

It's not that I was in search of a dad; I was okay with mine not being present, and on the contrary, his absence left a blank slate on which I could write my own rules of how to be a good father. My desire to become a gentleman from an early age, objectively learning how to become a strong and independent man, and more importantly, a great father, without a role model or direct male influence, has granted me a unique perspective that I've been repeatedly, and even insistently, encouraged to share.

I've decided to tell my story because I believe the greatest gifts a father can give his child are the cornerstones—time, guidance, wisdom, and love— upon which to build a life of his or her choosing.

For more than three decades, I built my own

cornerstones, learning from great men like Arnold Palmer, the golf legend and philanthropist, for whom I worked over a twelve-year period. He was a man who lived life with integrity and kindness, and was one of the greatest American success stories—the groundskeeper's son who became known as "The King" of the sport he loved so much. As part of Mr. Palmer's team, I keenly observed and admired the way he approached the game he loved and how he interacted with people. He taught me about the difference between success and winning, and about the parts of life that matter most: relationships, kindness, and helping people. To me, he was living proof that good guys win.

During a Fred Rogers conference for early childhood development on behalf of Arnold Palmer's charitable foundation in 2017, I spoke about being present as a father and shared how I'd taught my then two-year-old son Åsmund how to listen with his heart. After the conference, a senior executive woman from a big tech company came up to me and said, "I wish you were my dad." I'll never forget that. She told me how my perspective could change people's lives and that I should consider writing a book.

And so I began writing a memoir called *Four for Forty* and am nearly halfway done, but every day it gnaws at me to publish a book on fatherhood and my experience being my son Åsmund's "Baba." He was never able to pronounce Papa and he didn't call me Dad, so I've become known as simply Baba, which means Father in several other languages and cultures. *Four for Forty* is far more in-depth than this milieu novella, but the importance of this book, what it's really about, is what transpires when you spend uninterrupted time with your child to explore simply being together, phone free— amongst a nature backdrop.

One of the best pieces of parenting advice I ever received is "Only you really know your child." For me to deepen my understanding of my son, I've made a concerted effort to get on the same wavelength as him, to kill time together, to understand how to feel together. To see the world from his point of view and illustrate my world view, all the while leaving it open to discussion and wonderment.

I learned about feelings from watching *Mr. Rogers' Neighborhood,* one of my favorite shows as a child. He helped me understand that everyone is an individual, each person unique, and each with their own feelings. "One thing is certain," Mr. Rogers once said. "Children need lots of free, quiet time to get used to all that's developing within them. Have you noticed that unhurried time by yourself or with someone you really trust can be the best setting for your own personal growth? It's no different for children."

And there it is, so simple and so true.

I hope reading this novella of our little Adirondack adventure inspires you to take some time with your child—to make quiet memories together. To get closer than you have ever been before. To clear your mind and calm your nerves so your imaginations can take flight on a cool mountain breeze together. To author your life story as the parent you want your child to remember and tell tales about.

Welcome to *The Flying Sabuki*.

CHAPTER 1

THE FLYING SABUKI IS BORN

As we zip past rows of conifers, winding our way through the Adirondack Park, my soon-to-be six-year-old son, Åsmund, breaks the silence.

"Baba, do you know what a Flying Sabuki is?" he coolly asks.

Until yesterday, I didn't know what a Flying Sabuki is. I'll bet you don't know what one is either, and in my forty-two years on this earth, I never imagined how much better my life would be with them in it. Luckily, Åsmund had plenty of time to tell me on our ten-hour drive from our home in Shaker Heights, OH to our vacation destination, Camp Kidura, located on Upper Saranac Lake, in upstate New York.

The beautiful all-timber frame peg and post structure has a quintessential Adirondack look to its architectural design and has a large companion boathouse with a rooftop patio nestled right on the lake. The experience of staying here encompasses one in solitude, tranquility, and quiet; an idyllic setting to rejuvenate the senses and restore one's spirits.

I've been coming up to the Camp at least once a year for over ten years now. There is something so close to the human soul that vibrates from all the life and unspoiled wilderness that are the Adirondacks. I can see why William James Stillman, an artist, writer, and skilled woodsman, fell in love with the area, and in 1858, created what came to be known as the Philosopher's Camp at Follensby Pond. The ten men of that group most notably included two poets, Ralph Waldo Emerson and James Russell Lowell, and two scientists, Louis Agassiz and Jeffries Wyman. The concept of a Philosopher's Camp has captured my imagination and fueled a thirst for introspective enlightenment that only unfettered time amongst the wild can manifest. *The Flying Sabuki* is born from our own father and son version of the Philosopher's Camp.

Nature is more than the trees, wind, rain, mountains, and seas—it is also the very pulse of our own stories as humans. Over the last one hundred years, we as a society have experienced a steady disconnection with the natural world itself, and perhaps we have forgotten that we, too, are simply a part of nature. Richard Louv coined the phrase "Nature Deficit Disorder" in his book "Last Child in the Woods," citing it as not a medical diagnosis, but rather the ultimate costs from our alienation from nature. Feeling the natural world, all senses engaged and feeding data to the brain, opens up the atavistic multi-generational subconscious that is hard-wired into our DNA, gently and subtly guiding us toward our true self. It is in this vein that I can think of no better place to write a book about fatherhood than here at Camp Kidura.

My friends Karim, Allie, and their family created the Camp and rent it to families who enjoy a getaway in a natural setting with comfortable and modern amenities. When we first met and became friends, we bartered a stay at the Camp for me to design the logo. The meaning of the brand icon I designed for the Camp is an artistic representation of the Egyptian symbol of Maat, a feather that is weighed against your life to determine which afterworld you'll enter. It also represents the balance of the seasons. Being Egyptian, Karim loved it. I'm proud to know my design work greets all visitors as they first enter the home. I have found that the Camp and the unbridled nature of the Adirondacks are a salve that, when applied in earnest for at least a week, provides an environment to gain reflective clarity and balance for life.

We came up to the Camp as a family when Åsmund was one year old, and then again for his fifth birthday, almost a year ago now, during some of the first months of Covid lockdown and shortly after leaving my career working for Arnold Palmer. We bonded for two weeks together as a family with our dogs Saoirse and Santtu. One of our favorite memories from that trip was the game "Slamwich," which we played in the third-floor crow's nest hundreds of times.

Åsmund has been counting down the days until vacation for weeks now, telling anyone and everyone that he was going to the Camp on vacation with his Baba.

Every day on the ride to school this past week, he and I would discuss what we were going to pack. Everything from his favorite sweatshirts to our matching t-shirt sets, to the plethora of games we wanted to bring. The games are massively important. Åsmund loves games.

"Baba, I think we should definitely bring

'Slamwich,' 'Stratego' cards, 'Uno,' and 'Battleship'."

"All great choices. How about we bring 'Kaleva' too?" I say.

"Yes! I like that because we can play lots of games quickly."

This is Åsmund's first spring break in Kindergarten and our first father and son trip up to the Camp by ourselves. Having two full weeks, my wife Tina and I decided that I'd take him up to the Camp for the first full week and he'd spend the next week with her at Acorn Adventure Academy, the nature preschool she owns and operates. Tina didn't have a solid father figure growing up either, and she's all for the two of us spending quality time together.

Being slightly older parents, I'm grateful for the extra years of life experience, earned wisdom, and patience. I like to measure personal, marriage, family, parenting, career, friends, hobbies, etc. on a scale of surviving to thriving, frequently taking stock in how to manage my mindshare and time in order to keep the needle dialed up on thriving.

I had hoped to one day be able to spend quality time at the Camp with my son, if I were to ever have a family of my own, ever since I first came up to the Camp with a bunch of my close friends. So to say this week here is a dream come true is unequivocally true.

The road trip from Cleveland to Upstate NY is about ten hours. For all those parents wondering how you take a five-year-old on a long road trip successfully without answering "Are we there yet?" several hundred times is a simple game of managing expectations, some activity books, and engaging conversation. Åsmund and I make great time on our journey, stopping for breakfast about forty-five minutes in, a fuel and bathroom break, a snack and bathroom break, and our final stop two hours away from the Camp in Watertown, NY, my favorite symbol of "you're almost there," Jean's Beans.

Jean's Beans is a classic family-owned little takeout eatery that has been serving some of the best fish, shrimp, oysters, scallops, and chicken since 1953. We promptly put in our order for a shrimp dinner and kids' meal (chicken nuggets & fries w/ homemade brownie) and then make our way to the sides. Jean's Beans' homemade macaroni salads in three flavors—tuna, shrimp, and regular—are a requirement for the full experience. The main event for Åsmund and me follows—selecting a half dozen of the biggest, most delicious yeast donuts we've ever seen. He chooses the two with "lellow" sprinkles and "gween" sprinkles. He can actually enunciate "yellow" and "green" correctly, but chooses to still say them with his little-boy voice. It's so insatiably cute, I don't harp on him to change it just yet. I appreciate that he enjoys being a kid as long as he can. Tina and I aren't going to rush him and we want him to imagine, play, and develop his sense of wonder.

"These are the best chicken nuggets and fries in the whole wide world!" Åsmund bellows from the back seat while chewing. "The best ever!"

I peer in the rearview mirror and see him looking out the window, really taking in the land-scape while eating. We embark on the best part of the drive up North. From Jean's Beans on up to the Camp, we drive through the Adirondack Park along windy tree-lined roads that are in great shape, which make for pure touring pleasure for my old manual '06 BMW 325xi, whose timeworn stiff sport suspension grips them with ease. It's just plain fun driving. Åsmund has asked me several times along the trip about the various kinds of cars he sees and asks what kind we have. He's glad we have *The Ulti-mate Driving Machine* and has also been keenly interested in the speed limit and why cars are breaking the laws driving too fast. I always drive the speed limit. I put safety first, and frankly, just don't want an out-of-state ticket.

It's been silent for about 15 minutes as we wind our way through the Adirondack Park, and then the best two-hour conversation I've had in years begins, and this book received its name.

"Baba, do you know what a Flying Sabuki is?"

"No, I don't. Please enlighten me," I say, grinning ear to ear.

"Well, it's a boulder that grows two googley eyes and wings—looks like a dragon."

"Whoa!"

"Yeah, Flying Sabuki eat rocks."

"They're cannibals?" I replied.

"What's a cannibal, Baba?"

"That's a living thing that eats other living things of the same species." I try to explain it in a simple way for him. This is an important talent you develop as a parent: boiling something down to its essence with the simplest words possible.

"Oh, well, yeah, then. It poops rocks too, and vomits rocks!" he says, giggling. Poop is pure comedic entertainment for a five-year-old.

"So Flying Sabuki have a closed-loop existence. What a circle of life. Amazing!"

Åsmund then goes on to tell me about the different species of Flying Sabuki. There are ones that shape-shift to look like a human shape, ones that are ice dragons, ones that are Chinese dragons, and all are made of rock.

"When they circle and wave their arms around, they're able to make a portal and go anywhere in time." In my rearview mirror, I can see him waving his arms in circles in front of him, his eyes wide with excitement.

"Every time a human goes through the portal, it goes to the mountains across the lake 'from the Camp," he says, referring to our destination. "Or it takes you somewhere you don't know. Or a place you think of in your mind. Like back to the dinosaurs, before the dinosaurs even lived, back to when the volcanoes were made... or to ancient Egypt. Flying Sabuki turn into their rock shape when humans are around and it's unlikely you'll ever see one, but some children, they're okay with." I'm trying to watch the road and my rearview mirror at the same time so I can witness his imaginative mind racing, creating a world he sees and is so excited to share with me.

"They love nature," he says. "Playing with trees and hugging trees. The trees are their friends."

I know exactly where that statement comes from. Åsmund went to Acorn Adventure Academy for his preschool life. My wife Tina and I couldn't find a preschool we liked, one that balanced imagination, play, outdoor adventures, environmental stewardship, etiquette, sharing, understanding your emotions, and academics—so she started one in our home. We wanted him to be in a loving home with peers and going out to experience nature, not in an institution situated within four walls.

The preschool experience Tina created showed him that he's a part of an expansive natural world that he can discover. Åsmund spent his earliest years hiking, exploring creeks and waterfalls, and developing an appreciation for Mother Nature. He grew up with a thirst for knowledge and a love for learning new things by going to the Natural History Museum, the Cleveland Orchestra, the Cleveland Museum of Art, and the Cleveland Metroparks. He couldn't have done that in a proverbial box eight hours a day. He now intrinsically understands the world is full of life and places to explore. He has a thriving imagination and desire to do things, with very little interest in screen-based devices.

I think we as a society place too little value on the nurturing of the human imagination and too much value on a child's ability to regurgitate facts. Being able to imagine a better world is what changes the world. I'm often astonished by how quickly our educational institutions strip our little ones of imagination by defining what is and isn't real. I'm a big fan of Sir Ken Robinson. I saw him once speak at The Cleveland Foundation about how education kills creativity, and I'm inclined to agree. Tina and I place a very high value on Åsmund's imagination and have to actively defend and protect it with ardent discipline in our current world—during the age of information.

One of the greatest compliments I received this year was from a colleague and fellow writer. It was in a division meeting where we had to say something nice about each of our co-workers. She said I have an imagination. For a forty-two-year-old brand and marketing executive, this was one of the greatest compliments I could receive. It meant this well-read twenty-something fiction writer thought I was plumb creative. My new boss said he thought I was a great father. This was a business meeting that I'll not soon forget, having new colleagues that I'd only been working with for several months acknowledge two things that I hope so much to embody.

It gave me hope for Åsmund to keep his imagination and I know he will when we do things like going to Camp Kidura for a week just to be together, describing the nature around us, telling stories with our StoryWorld cards at night, building an epic Lego pirate ship, and killing time together chit-chatting, as we like to say.

Åsmund and I have an easy understanding of each other. We feel connected and in sync with one another. To me, there's nothing better in this world than the bond between a father and his son. It makes the hard things in life so much easier. It makes trust intrinsic, and love pervasive and paramount over anything else.

"Look at that King Sabuki!" Åsmund blurts out during the final minutes of our drive down Panther Road in the Wawbeek area. "He's rolled up in a giant ball!"

He's glorious in scale at about thirty feet in diameter. One of the great natural phenomena of the Adirondacks are the massive granite boulders strewn about the landscape, left from the last ice age as glaciers receded and melted. This particular King Sabuki is right next to the road before we turn down to enter the Sekon group of Camps.

Down the old dirt road we drive after nearly ten hours on the road.

"So many Flying Sabuki, Baba!"

There are granite boulders a-plenty lining the road as we approach the Camp.

"We're here! We're here!" he shouts.

I'm relieved to make it safely, and exhausted

from the last two hours of winding roads and speed limit changes going from 60 to 25 through little mountain lake towns.

It's civil twilight. Åsmund notes the smell of the air being fresh and we make our way down the raw, uneven granite steps with our Jean's Beans dinner and belongings. We make multiple trips unloading the car, the sound of snow and ice crunching beneath our feet with every step, so much more present to one's ears when there's no sound pollution. He's such a good helper. I'm ravenous, having not afforded myself the time to eat on the last leg of our journey so we could get here before nightfall. I don't like multi-tasking, especially when driving with precious cargo.

Walking in through the front door, you're greeted on the right by an open staircase with a railing made from tree branches, and in front of you is a great room with a hanging antler chandelier above cozy wool and leather couches huddled around a three-story granite fireplace. A warm amber light from lamps with birch bark shades, recessed lighting, and hanging lights bathe all the natural wood and granite as you look out the wall of windows onto the lake.

Immediately upon entering, Åsmund takes off his shoes and neatly places them next to the door.

"We need to keep their place clean and nice, right, Baba?"

"Yes, we do. It's so nice of Allie and Karim to let us stay here. We'll take care of it like it is our own home."

I love that instead of running in and checking everything out, his first thought is to take a moment to be polite and affirm that we'll be clean in our stay here.

Åsmund and I walk down the steps. He stands tall, hands in pockets, a reflective look on his face, and calmly says, "It's good to be back here. Right, Baba?"

"It sure is, Åsmund. I love it here."

"Me too," he says slowly and softly. After a pause, "It's so quiet and beautiful. I love you, Baba."

"I love you too," I say.

He gives my leg a hug and I get down on his level so we can have a big bear hug.

"We love hugs, don't we, Baba?"

"Yeah, we do; hugs are my favorite."

He helps me put away the cooler of groceries and I make us both a plate of Jean's Beans. He insists we sit next to each other on the bench side of the long rectangular wooden table that is situated in front of French doors that overlook a Flying Sabuki and the lake.

Popping his last chicken nuggets in his mouth, Åsmund bellows, "Let's start making those Legos! Bring in that box first." We empty nine bags containing 1,260 Lego pieces onto the big wooden dining table with him sitting on my lap on the long bench. A giant Flying Sabuki is perched on the shore sitting right outside our dining room sliding doors, which open up to a standing balcony. "I wanna climb that Flying Sabuki," he says, taking a moment between Lego steps to look outside. We walk over and open the doors. The view is captivating in its pure, frozen beauty. Upper Saranac Lake whispers it's timeless wisdom for those who care to listen. The brisk winter mountain air seems to calm our lungs and relax our shoulders as we continue to unwind.

After ten years of coming up here, my first night at the camp usually has a tinge of anxiety, as if the hectic world that I just came from doesn't want to release its sharp claws from my consciousness. It demands that my mind and thoughts remain prisoner on the endless hamster wheel that is modern middle-class American life. I've learned to let that only take the first night. When I first came to Camp Kidura, it took me several days to relax enough to feel the sense of freedom I now experience the moment I arrive in this wild, beautiful place.

Åsmund and I get three bags into making the Lego pirate ship. We share half a donut. "This is the best donut on the planet, Baba," he says. I'm beginning to realize that everything is the best just because it's right here and right now, distraction free. Cell phones don't work up here, and that's part of the magic.

With Åsmund so proud of his solid start for the Lego pirate ship, it's a great breaking point for bedtime. We get into our shower made with stone walls where water directly from the lake outside our window cleanses us. The floors in the bathroom and house are heated from within by water from the lake. It's an incredible technological system that makes for a supremely cozy cabin.

He climbs up into a wooden bed that has a tree branch canopy and soft cotton sheets. "This is sooooooo cozy, Baba!" he squeaks, getting under the poofy white down comforter. "It's crazy cozy."

We pull out one of his new books, titled *Museum Trip*. It's a book with no words, only pictures, for which you can tell your own story. Åsmund and I love this kind of book, and he goes first and tells his version and then I tell mine. It's a wonderful story.

We click the nightstand lamp off and snuggle in for a long winter's nap.

"I wish it was morning already, Baba. I love you."

"I love you, too," I reply, my eyes welling up with unfathomable joy. No words can and never will encompass the sea of love I feel for my boy. His little hand clenches my shirt and I feel his breath slow as he drifts off to sleep, the weight of his little body tucked safely in my right arm like we always do. These are the moments that make fatherhood so profoundly moving.

CHAPTER 2

LEGOS, WRITING & LAKE PLACID

I can't help but submit to the natural circadian rhythm that Camp Kidura presents me with each and every morning. The Camp is situated facing the east and I wonder how the sun will greet us from behind the lake and mountain that hold the horizon, the main stage of the Camp. The father and son snuggle-bears, as we like to say, are greeted on our first morning when the warm rays of the sun bear down on us through our window. To crest or not to crest is the question that's answered outside the wall of windows at the foot of our bed, a daily performance by the sun at the Camp theatre.

Åsmund promptly gives me a big hug upon opening his eyes.

"How did you sleep?" he asks.

"I was pretty hot. You?"

"Me too. This room is hot!"

We tossed and turned throughout the night. The in-floor heating really pumps in the southeast bedroom. We decide we'll sleep in the northeast bedroom the following night and immediately go to test out the bed. Super cozy.

He and I love co-sleeping, and if it were up to us, we would co-sleep most nights. We slept in the same bed for years together after our house burned down when he was two. We both found comfort falling asleep together reading books. Tina built him one of the coolest elevated kids' beds, which he loves to sleep in now. We still do storytime every night in my bed and then I say, "All aboard!" He jumps onto my back and I transfer him to his bunk bed. We've gotten used to it, and I really enjoy being able to read my own books before bed again. So books and passing out together at the Camp on vacation is a real treat.

Åsmund descends the stairs to the dining room table to pick up where he left off on the Lego pirate ship.

"Want a donut for breakfast?" I ask.

"Yeah, Baba! I can't believe it, a donut for breakfast!" Donuts for breakfast are a very special father and son treat. Tina doesn't like sweets. At all. She's one hundred percent savory, and any chance the boys get for a special sweet treat is savored.

I begin frying up a pound of bacon on the heartily seasoned iron griddle. Bacon and donuts, the breakfast of Camp Kidura champs.

"We're going to write a book about our time here," I say while we're eating.

"So cool! You can write chapter one while I do Legos." he quips back. "Why do you want to write a book?"

"Do you remember what you did yesterday?"

"No."

"That's why."

He nods in affirmation. I feel the lump in my throat build and my eyes well up. I fight hard to keep my words unwaveringly solid in the next part of my reply. "Because one day, I won't be here, and you're going to read this and remember how much we enjoyed spending time together."

"I understand, Baba," he says with a little well in his eyes too.

I know he is thinking about a few nights ago when he came to the realization that I won't be alive for his entire life. He had asked before bed what we would do together in fifty years and I told him the honest truth that I may or may not be alive when I'm ninety-two. His little lip quivered, and he said, "You're going to die?" I went on to explain average life expectancy, the circle of life, and how important it is for us to make the time we spend together special. He gave me the biggest hug.

"Chapter one should be about Flying Sabuki and Legos, Baba!" He changes the tone to excitement. "You sit across from me and watch me build the pirate ship and type the story. I can help if you have questions."

For the next couple hours, I plucked the keys of my Qwerkywriter S mechanical typewriter keyboard Tina had gotten me for Christmas. My writing process and joy derived from writing is directly attributed to my chosen typing device. Just like when I play piano, the action and feel is monumentally important to the art created from it. I normally use an actual typewriter for first drafts. Åsmund and I have matching 1956 Royal Quiet Deluxe typewriters that we type on. Mine is a matte mint green and his is a shiny cherry red.

I'm probably one of the last people that learned how to type on a mechanical typewriter in 7th grade when I fell in love with writing on one. *Hemingway* became my compatriot in vigorously stamping my thoughts onto paper three years ago. I try my best not to use the delete button while writing this on my computer to preserve the forward motion. I have, however, missed the visceral experience of manual typing, outside the data stream, pushing the carriage return with purpose and loading new pages as I watch my work stack up to my right.

Two years ago, I came up to the Camp in the fall for a solo writing retreat with *Hemingway* and punched 40,000 words of the first draft of my full-length memoir, written like I'm speaking to Åsmund. Last year, for Åsmund's fifth birthday at the Camp, I gave him his red Royal quiet deluxe accompanied by a typed letter from his Baba inside. A typewriter is a great way to teach writing letters and sentences. It's a very specific fine motor skill to press the keys and it's distraction-free, compared to a computer or tablet.

The Qwerkywriter S keyboard has made an excellent teammate on our trip. I write twenty-three hundred words (or nearly ten pages) as we listen to music and build our playlist for the book. The hit track I had found to start us off is "Family" by Drew Holcomb & The Neighbors. Such a fun song that we had to dance and run around to. Åsmund got through bags 4 and 5 of the Lego pirate ship.

"That deserves an 'Atta boy' alright," I say. We're

both now invested in our projects and are encouraging one another. Our individual and mutual success running in tandem is how we'll accomplish our goals.

Both satisfied with our progress, we decide to go explore outside the Camp. It's a gorgeous sunny day with the temperature in the fifties. There are Flying Sabuki everywhere. Åsmund climbs up the nearest one, and upon reaching top, declares, "This is the grandpa Flying Sabuki. It's ginormous!"

Åsmund loves climbing. We have a membership to the Shaker Rocks rock gym at home and he has his own gear. He's a complete natural that would draw a crowd when climbing the adult walls. He went straight to the top of a fifty-foot wall on his first attempt—fearless.

In the natural environment, he exercises his ascent of the Flying Sabuki with safety, caution, and precision, calculating each and every foot and hand hold. It's a pleasure to watch. There is a fine line here as a father, wanting to make sure he's safe and providing the room for growth. I encourage him to take his time and find his line before starting, look for your hand and foot holds. His instructor at the rock gym would marvel at his natural ability, especially the time he hung with one arm, shaking off the ache in the other before leaping up to his next hand hold—my little guy can climb. In my mind, I time travel back to my youth, recalling my great love of climbing, and imagining the thrill my younger self would have had scaling the walls of the rock gym or this beautiful granite Flying Sabuki.

He identifies a "Baby Sabuki" and "Mommy Sabuki" before going round to the lake side of the Camp to discover a "King Sabuki." He climbs the King Sabuki, mapping and deliberating his route verbally, discussing the stability of the melting snow with me, before making the successful ascent.

"Take my picture on top of this King Flying Sabuki, Baba!"

Picture taken. Memory made.

"Are you having a good day, Baba?" Åsmund asks as we come back inside the Camp.

"I'm having the best day ever!" I reply enthusiastically.

"Me too! This is the best day ever." We hug.

I take my shower while he works on more Legos before embarking on our journey to Lake Placid for toys, games, books, and provisions.

"I'll bring my camera so I can take pictures of the mountains and trees!" Åsmund announces just before leaving. He has a little blue and yellow digital camera that's just his size and takes low-res photos. He revels in all the pine trees along the road and the view of snow-capped mountains in the distance over the crest of hills, snapping pictures with purpose.

We talk through what order we are going to do things in Lake Placid. It will be 1:45 when we arrive and want to make the most of our time. First and foremost would be a trip to the toy store Imagination Station in the center of town.

"Look at that!" he yells, entering the store and pointing to a ball about the size of my hand that is pitted with thumbnail-sized circles. It's a hyper bouncy ball called a Waboda Moon Ball. Super cool.

"We're definitely getting it," I say decisively. A bouncy ball is a classic toy that I know will result in hours of fun at the Camp.

One of the absolute best parts of fatherhood is being able to zealously shop in a toy store knowing you can buy anything you want (within reason). It's so refreshing being a kid again and I wish there were more toy stores. We're having an awesome time shopping and exploring all the expertly curated toys and games.

Åsmund and I are two of a pair in that we both lead with a smile and have no hesitation striking up a conversation with strangers. "My Baba and I love telling stories," he says to a little girl about four years old. We're looking at a game called "Stories of the Three Coins," which we quickly decide is a must have. The mom gives us this look like "why are you talking to her," then catches herself and realizes it's just a little kid talking to another little kid. Jeez, folks, we're in a toy store; it's okay to be friendly, even with our COVID-19 pandemic masks on. Her mom suggests the game to her and the little girl yells at her mom, "I want to pick out my own toys!"

Åsmund looks at me and says, "She's not very nice. That's not how you get toys, right, Baba?"

"Correct, son. We work together to choose our toys and games."

"Right."

We press on and he discovers a game called "Triple Cross." Looks fun and the price is right. We take our three toy treasures and check out, so excited for the fun ahead of us when we return to Camp.

Time for lunch at the Adirondack Brewing Company. I'm hoping they have their amazing Beef Wellington on the menu, but it's a shortened menu for COVID dining. Burger for me, fries and lemonade for Åsmund. Delicious. "We sure worked up an appetite toy shopping, didn't we?"

"Toy shopping makes me hungry! I love fries and toys, Baba."

Now for a trip to The Book Store Plus. It's a beautifully merchandised bookshop that also has art supplies. We always have a great time in the bookstore and go almost every weekend, when at home, to either Loganberry Books on Larchmere or Horizontal Books on W. 25th Street in Ohio City when we go to the West Side Market.

He quickly beelines his way to the back where the children's books are located. He'd love it if I compared him to a dog sniffing out food. Åsmund loves dogs and it's no coincidence that the first book he identifies is entitled *Snow Friends* by Margery Cuyler with a picture of a boy and his dog on the cover. I kneel down next to him and read it.

"Let's definitely get this one, Baba!" he exuberantly declares for all to hear after I say, "The End." It's an adorable book about a boy whose dog goes on a winter walk without his owner and meets a friend. They're eventually reunited with their kid owners with lots of kisses and they all become snow friends.

We meander around the corner and I see a book peeking out from behind another entitled *The Wisdom of Trees* and I surmise at a glance this will be a hit. One of his most favorite books is one I got him for Christmas several years ago called *The Universe is a Tree*. I flip through a few pages with him, and he's immediately sold. "Let's get it!" Although he tends to pronounce "let's" as "yits" every now and then, channeling his inner toddler, I don't correct him. It's fun to see his innocent excitement over a book about the wisdom of trees and how they work together to form a natural kingdom.

He pulls out *A Year Around the Great Oak* by Gerda Muller on a shelf his height. I've always thought bookstores could come up with a more innovative way to display books at a child's height with a little interactive mechanical engineering. I've always wished it would work like an endless dry cleaner's rack.

"We have an oak tree in our yard, Baba!" he says. "It's sacred." He gets that from *The Universe is a Tree* book. I agree. Oak trees hold a special magic and presence about them. It was one of the reasons I fell in love with our home; the backyard has a large oak where I hung a swing I made for him. This Dutch children's book author has put together a spectacular story around an oak tree and includes an awesome reference section in the back. Åsmund loves reference books. He always has, even as a toddler. From dinosaurs, to sea life, to one of his favorites, *Mythical Creatures*; if it's a spread or page presenting a singular concept that's part of a larger thematic, he's in.

With five minutes to spare on the meter, we head to the Price Chopper to get our week's worth of provisions. Given the opportunity to shop for ourselves for a week without input from Tina is a feeling of pure freedom, like anything is possible. We made a rudimentary list prior to leaving the Camp so we didn't forget the essentials. The rest is fair game.

"Let's go to the candy aisle!" he belts, pulling the cart immediately upon entering the Price Chopper. Candy holds the highest tier on the food chart in Åsmund's world. We've fortunately been able to work with him in a positive way for metered consumption without making it a reward. I really enjoyed the book *Rewards and Punishments* by Alfie Cohn, which gave me some solid advice for how to navigate the potentially hazardous waters of treating a child like a dog with treats for doing something.

It's been really important to me as a father to teach him to hold himself accountable, especially when no one is watching. That's integrity. He's getting it too. We get to the candy aisle and he's clearly overwhelmed by all the choices. He's not really a big chocolate guy. He likes it, but it's not the be all end all. His favorite candy right now is probably Sour Patch Kids, and gummies are the standby go-to choice.

He chooses Scooby Snacks gummies and Sour Skittles.

"Two is plenty, right, Baba?"

"Sounds good, little buddy."

I don't need to limit him on candy; he's aware that he cannot overindulge. I so enjoy when all that hard work as a parent comes to fruition in a small moment like this.

Our final item is shampoo. I forgot it and the camp was out, which gave me the perfect opportunity for an olfactory adventure in the Price Chopper. We smell a half dozen or so shampoos and discuss what we smell, and then he finds one he likes: Old Spice Swagger.

"I love this smell, Baba! What's it called?"

"Old Spice Swagger."

"What's Swagger smell like?"

I'm practically giddy at the chance to teach him about my area of expertise, branding and marketing. "Swagger isn't a smell; it's a characteristic and feeling—it's confidence. It's that hitch in your step when you walk. The people that make this shampoo want you to feel that way so you'll buy it."

"Let's buy it!"

"So you want swagger, eh? Well, son, you've already got it. I remember how you used to sit when you were one year old; laid back, legs crossed with your arm up on the armrest on the couch, snackin' on some puffs... I said to Mommy, 'Look! He's got swagger!'"

He cracks a half smile.

"Sometimes they call it charisma too. You just have to be confident in who you are, creating your own life story, and remember what I've taught you."

"Okay, Baba," he says with conviction. He knows he's got charisma and swagger. "Let's get the shampoo. I still like how it smells."

I let out a hearty chuckle watching him walk down the aisle holding the shampoo, hitch in his step.

Two hundred and nine dollars later, we're back on the road headed to the Camp.

"What's your favorite element, Baba? Mine is wind. The wind is our friend," he says out of nowhere, his gaze in a trance watching the trees go by at 55 mph along NY Rt. 3 North.

"Mine is definitely water," I reply, my eyes glued to the mountain road. It can be harrowing driving up here on the curving roads. "Water and wind go well together."

"Yeah, they do, like for sailing the boat!"

"Heck yeah, Åsmund. That's why we've got *Escapade*—to go sailing."

"When wind and water come together, they can make ice, or wind can shift the clouds, and when there's no wind for the sails, I can make some wind for us to go," he says in a stream of conscious thought.

This past fall, I bought my first sailboat, a 1975 Ericson 29 sloop that my friends and I sailed down from Michigan. Åsmund and I have yet to take her sailing together, but we have spent a couple Saturdays on board playing and building Legos. He and I both can't wait to take an adventure to the Erie Islands and the Canadian sand dunes on the northeast shores of Lake Erie. This summer will be our first season on *Escapade,* and we're both counting down.

We turn onto Panther Road and slow down to look at a field of Flying Sabuki. It was an amazing sight, seeing hundreds of granite boulders littered across a steep hillside to our left, and to our right, a steep decline down to Upper Saranac Lake, and we pass a seventy-five-foot, or higher, granite boulder.

"There's a Triple King of Kings Flying Sabuki! Oh my god!" The scope and size of this boulder is awe-inspiring and there's a house sitting on top of it.

After I haul in all the groceries and they're put away, we start dropping the hyper bouncy ball off the balcony inside to see how high it will bounce. The hyper bouncy ball is just plain fun—until it gets stuck in the deer antler chandelier.

"Waaaaaaaaaa!" Tears erupt from Åsmund's eyes and he wails with the kind of emotional distress an adult would have at a dearly loved one's funeral.

"It's going to be okay, Åsmund. Baba has cleaned the chandelier before, and I can get it. Please don't cry, sweetie," I say in my most gentle voice. Åsmund is sensitive, like his dad, and feels deeply, even for bouncy balls. I could feel his pain, him thinking he would not be able to play with this most amazing of toys. "Help me find the brooms and we'll get it down. Let me show you how it works."

As soon as he understands there is a path to retrieval, the tears subside and he follows me around. We pull the chandelier over after several tries and loose the ball to a happy hooray!

Hyper balled out for a bit, we decide to go down to the boathouse game room to play a game of foosball. It's a gorgeous view of the water outside two double doors, and in the distance, we can see a small green house with a red roof nestled on the shore across the lake.

I make my first goal and his face goes straight and immediately changes to delight when the ball pops out on his side.

"Yay, the ball comes out right here!"

I'm amazed by his innocent non-competitive joy out of just learning to play this game. We play for the next thirty minutes and do a little shuffleboard before Tina calls us on Facetime to check in with her boys. There may not be cell service at the Camp, but the internet works well.

Back at the table while I catch up with Tina, he finishes off building the stern of the pirate ship just before dinner. He's making tremendous progress. I haven't put together a single piece of the entire ship. He's done it all himself and I'm so proud of him.

"Baba, the box says ages 9+. I'm almost six and I think we'll finish this tomorrow, won't we?!" he says, studying the box.

"You sure will! I'm so proud of you."

He holds out his arms, motioning for a hug. "Huggies!" he says. "When I make my arms go like this, that means I want a hug. We love hugs."

We do love hugs. I once read that the average person needs seventeen hugs a day for emotional equilibrium. I'm guessing most Americans don't get half that number. I'm lucky Åsmund is here for a hug anytime.

Dinner is remarkably simple; it's what Åsmund calls "noodle soups." He basically eats Maruchan Chicken Ramen soup every night for dinner and may deviate to a grilled cheese every now and then, but that's pretty much standard issue for this picky eater. When he was one to two years old, he would eat literally anything. Fois gras, heady cheese, zucchini—you name it, he ate it. Today, that seems like a distant golden age for his foodie mother and father.

It's getting late and approaching 9:00. He knows it too.

"Baba, you promised we'd play the new story game today," he says with a factual tone in his voice. I did promise. "Let's secret handshake on it." Our secret handshake had only just been born a week ago and consists of a fist bump, hammer bump where he hits my fist coming down with his, and then a high-five that explodes backwards. I just wrote an essay about it on my escurry.com blog. Every father and son needs a secret handshake. It's a symbol of your bond and only something the two of you have.

We set up and I read the instructions before beginning the "Stories of Three Coins" game. It's incredible! We tell one heck of a tale and I love that the game is cooperative and the objective is to get the happy ending. The world needs more kids' games like this.

And so the story of our first day at the Camp comes to an end.

We've got a lot more to write and more to explore.

I trust the Camp will guide us.

CHAPTER 3

OUR SHIP SETS SAIL

How lucky are we to wake up to a gorgeous sunrise? The spirit of the Adirondack mountains beams through our windows, beckoning us to come outside and experience its freedom and feel the crisp winter air. Åsmund snuggles in for hugs before bounding from bed.

"Yits eat breakfast!" he exclaims.

I fry up some bacon; the smell of maple-soaked meat permeates the cabin. He devours a thick slice with some Life cereal and apple cider. I prepare myself a nice breakfast of two eggs over easy with toast from Jean's Beans and Vermont butter, and of course, bacon.

Next up, Legos and writing. It's so nice to work

across from each other. Åsmund at his big boy age of five-and-a-half, still enjoys a game of peek-a-boo as he smiles over the laptop screen.

We get to work. He's so focused and now in the home stretch, having finished bags 7 and 8 of the pirate ship.

I'm in a groove writing and bang out thirty-three hundred words (nearly fourteen pages) of this book. Wow, did that feel good. It's not often back at home I can just sit and type on this luxurious keyboard for hours on end. What a treat. Typing for me is like therapy. I just love the feeling of words flowing from my fingers. The sensation and parts of my brain that are delighted is akin to playing the piano.

We take a break to go outside. This is one of our favorite things to do here at the Camp. We don't need to go far here to feel the majesty of Mother Nature; she's all around us. Time slows and I feel every moment with serene intensity.

"This is the most special portal," Åsmund says to me as he goes through a tree in the shape of a V that's between the giant granite wall and the boathouse. The last time we were here for his birthday, we played this same game. I jump down and go through the portal with him.

I think the weight of parenthood and the many

responsibilities of American adult life can make it difficult to give in to the simple act of opening our imagination and playing with our children. When I'm here at Camp Kidura, I don't have that weight and digital distractions in the palm of my hand. The place itself is a character, wielding its opinion through quiet, subtle cues that are easily heard if one is willing to listen.

Åsmund comes flying by me through the tree.

"I just went back in time before the earth was born and there was just nature, right?!" he says in a statement, capping it with a one-worded question for validation.

"Right!" I retort with zeal, trying to imagine what he's seeing. He's clearly seeing and imagining what that might look like; his dark brown eyes are darting from left to right.

"Look through this portal," Åsmund says. "I just made a friend named Drago. We went back in time to before rocks were born."

What an awesome break. I wish my work breaks were like this every day. How different my days would be if writing was my profession. I would write on *Escapade* during the summer, take a break for a sail or swim, and continue writing after a fresh cup of coffee. In the winter, it would be a cozy cabin with a view of a lake. Water is my element and also my muse.

While we were quietly working at the table on Legos and writing, I heard a rumbling in the distance. Having been up here so many times, I knew that sound did not belong. It began to increase in amplitude, and before I knew it, I saw a military chopper flying slowly south fifty feet over the frozen lake. Åsmund said he saw its sound crack the ice on the lake below it. I look out at the frozen lake and indeed there is a large new crack in the ice. Then I remember Fort Drum is located near here.

"That doesn't belong here." Åsmund notes. "It's not part of nature."

We write and Lego more.

This is the good stuff in life, sitting across the table from my son, writing a book for him while he plays Legos.

We go Flying Sabuki climbing for a break after some hyper bouncy ball. I've heard it a hundred times now. "Hyper bouncy ball... hyper!" He bounces the ball on that last hyper and then attempts to catch it.

After our break, he finishes the Lego pirate ship. Interestingly, he lets the final anchor and bowsprit linger in its completion. Then he consciously chooses to finish it.

I thought he would be elated, jumping up and down marveling at all his hard work coming to a culmination, but not Åsmund. The look on his face is stoic with a hint of somber. I think he's sad that it's over. I imagine I'll feel the same way when I finish editing and publishing this book.

"You did it!" I exclaim. A smile starts to appear on his face. "Let's check it out."

We look over all the details and play with the pirates. His favorite part of the entire project is the multi-colored abstract-shaped figurehead for the ship. It's unique, colorful, and I can see why he likes it. It's the one element of the project that leaves room for imaginative interpretation. The rest is all very literal and a mirror of the real world. But not the bow figurehead. In that moment, I can envision Åsmund becoming a unique figurehead. I hope this young man, who is so in touch with the natural world around him and the people who populate it, will be an agent of change for our future world.

I'm reminded that I might not have noticed that small figurehead detail had we been at home. His reaction to finishing the biggest project he's ever undertaken as an individual helped me understand him as a person. He put together 1,200+ pieces all by himself. I didn't touch a single brick or help in the assembly. I only helped him locate a piece if he had trouble finding it. He made it known from the very beginning he would do it all himself. I'm not sure you can teach the spirit of self-determination. I know this kind of stick-to-itiveness can transcend into all areas of life and I'm happy and proud to see it manifest at such a young age.

I stage a little photo session and have him stand on a chair and triumphantly hold his pirate ship up high while I take his photo. He beams with pride and so do I.

It's dinner time and I begin to cook chicken on the iron griddle while he invents a dragon card game with ten cards on each side. He repeatedly calls me over to say which of my dragons will attack which of his. The best part of this game is the rules, or should I say the lack thereof. He imagines who wins battles based on no logical markings on the card like numbers or letters. I explain what they mean—King, Queen, Jack, Ace, etc.—but he's not interested. *Know your audience*, I think to myself. He's playing! I'm certainly not going to get in the way of this game, and he ends up winning, naturally.

The chicken is done grilling, and it's time to put together my Camp Kidura Chicken Casserole recipe. I love a good noodle-based casserole, and I make them often; they're hearty and reheat well.

Here's the recipe I came up with on the fly:

1/2 box of penne boiled

2 chicken breasts coated in your favorite spice seasoning—mine is Penzey's Northwoods grilled—and sliced into bite-size pieces. Your choice of spice combination can determine the flavor of the dish.

2 cans of Campbell's Cream of Chicken soup with herbs

1/2 cup of milk

1/4 of cream

1/2 bag of NY sharp cheddar, jack, and swiss cheese

2/3 stick of butter melted combined with smashed Triscuits

Combine all ingredients except cheese and Triscuits in a glass baking pan. Spread cheese on top and bake at 350 degrees for 15 minutes. Remove and add Triscuit crumb topping and bake for another 10-15 minutes or until bubbling. Let rest for 15 minutes before serving.

While the casserole was cooking, Åsmund and I were standing on the balcony observing the stars in the clear night sky. It's brisk out, but not cold. He breaks the silence.

"Baba, can you put on the song 'Way Back When?'" It's a song by a band called Grizfolk that he heard at the end of the *Peabody and Sherman* movie. I put it on and Åsmund closes his eyes and really listens to it. He's bobbing and swaying his head to the song, lost in it. I follow suit and we bob our heads to the beat and relish in the amazing sound of this inspiring song. I love everything about the musicality of the song and the lyrics are befitting of our father-son Camp experience.

After the song is over, I stop the music and pause. Åsmund's sense of hearing is activated.

"I can hear the water moving where there is no ice." he says in a whisper.

You can indeed hear the water gently lapping against the shore where it's melted.

There are times when I wonder, *How am I so lucky to be able to live with this little person with such a beautiful soul?*

I feel a little lump in my throat as he leans against my leg. We're just looking at the lake in silence.

It's time for showers, and afterward, I say, "Let's read our bedtime books over a bowl of Neapolitan ice cream with chocolate sauce." It's almost like he can't believe his ears; his eyes light up in shock and awe at my proposal. This is not something we would do at home, and that's the point.

We make our sundaes and I read him *King Brid-good's in the Bathtub,* and we have tons of laughs over the King wanting to do everything from lunch, fishing, and a masquerade ball in his tub. In the end, the Page finally figures out how to get the King out of the bathtub. He simply pulls the plug. The illustrations are so vivid with detail and warrant careful examination.

Then it's a heartwarming reading of *Snow Friends,* and we retreat to bed and look forward to another day at Camp.

CHAPTER 4

HUNGRY FOR LIFE

We're greeted with yet another gorgeous morning sunrise. It's odd this time of year for the weather to be so sunny up in the Adirondacks. Even the cashier at the Price Chopper noted to us that we picked the first week of good weather to come up. If you're one who likes weather like these ardent northerners do, you can truly appreciate the climate throughout the forty-six high peaks.

Åsmund starts the day craving breakfast and "Life." I love that we made his default cereal "Life" cereal so he can start his day with the best double entendre ever.

"I'm hungry for life, Baba!" he yelps, bouncing

up and down, and pulling me out from under our big Snoopy fleece blanket that we brought with us for that touch of home comfort. He careens himself down the stairs, running for his "Life." (I can't resist the future dad joke.)

After our heartiest big breakfast thus far, we debate taking apart the Lego pirate ship. I make sure he doesn't want to play with it more, and indeed, he's ready to move on to the next challenge, Skull Island.

"It sure comes apart more quickly than putting it together, doesn't it, Åsmund?"

"Boy, are there a lot of pieces! Did you ever have a Lego set this big when you were a kid?"

"No, the biggest set I had was the one right there in that box we brought."

"So you didn't have to do 20 or 10 or 4 times parts?" He's referring to the quantity of pieces required when doing different steps in the instructions.

"No, I would build with what I had and still enjoyed hours of fun with Legos," I reply in an equally matter-of-fact-sounding voice.

"I'm lucky to have a set this big."

"Yes, you are."

He has started to understand value recently, asking how much it cost when we picked it out and ordered it together online. I remember him belting out, "Wow that's a lot!" when I told him ninety-nine dollars. It is a lot, but the reason for the cost becomes evident to me, given the amount of R&D that went into creating this 3-in-1 set, as we take apart the ship.

The sheer number of tiny little pieces in such an array of shapes, each with their own purpose, spread out over this giant table. I quickly realize there is no way he can build anything else unless there's some semblance of organization to this field of plastic chaos. We embark on taking apart each and every one of the 1,200+ pieces and organize them by color, shape, and function.

This project takes the entire morning and this book has to take a back seat to getting him organized and back in the groove to build something new.

"Time for a Flying Sabuki climbing break." Åsmund announces. It's so fun watching him climb the granite formations just outside and adjacent to the Camp. These are memories I know he'll have forever. Memories that are deeply embedded within his consciousness, to touch and smell the earth. My memory of climbing down the limestone cliff to the Grand River near my childhood home in Fairport Harbor, Ohio is still with me thirty years later. I can still feel the limestone in my hands, the smell of mud and fish, the sound of the river flowing—when you engage all your senses in nature as a child you're forever connected to it.

Our first nap time at the Camp was glorious. Just glorious. The sun beams through the windows as if giving us a firm nudge, "You shouldn't be sleeping now." And Åsmund and I defiantly saying, "But, darn it, we're tired and choose to not just relax, but to rest."

After our nap, he quietly sets to work on building the small boat for Skull Island, popping some Scooby Snacks in his mouth between steps.

He's been craving orange juice all day and I suggest we go into Tupper Lake to pick up dinner and get some orange juice from the gas station. McDonald's Happy Meal for him and homemade pesto fettuccine and garlic knots for me from Little Italy. Vacation is about favorite things, right? Going on that belief, nuggets and pasta are a dreamy dinner for this father-son duo.

The spotting of Flying Sabuki on Panther Mountain Road don't disappoint on our way back home. He's lovingly identifying King Sabuki from regular Sabuki and baby Sabuki. Magic and possibility are everywhere in Åsmund's mind.

This is intentional. While other kids might be

told what's real and not real when their child asks questions like "Are dragons real?" I tend to reply with a question like "Do you think it's possible for them to be real?" I want him to come to his own conclusions with questions like that.

Who's to say they've never been real or if quantum physics and the possibility of multiple worlds intersecting or the multiverse working in ways we have no comprehension of made them real at some point during human existence? Aren't many myths based on some shred of reality? Isn't our perception of reality that of the observer? Trying to weave some basic modern non-material science and quantum mechanics type questions into his life I believe will result in future fresh eyes and thinking.

We hunker down in the sunroom off the balcony and watch the *Big Foot Family* movie and eat our dinner together. Åsmund and I both loved the first one called *Son of Bigfoot,* not only for the story, animation, and voices, but because of the soundtrack. A Belgium band trio by the name of "Puggy" wrote the soundtrack, and it's beautiful. We listen to it all the time. It's definitely in his Spotify "aisle," as he likes to say. He knows it's a playlist, yet chooses to call it an aisle. I love that.

He sits in my lap under a blanket and we finish the movie, then as promised with a secret handshake, we play "Stories of the Three Coins"—twice. This time, I hit record in the audio app on my iPhone and capture that adorable little voice as we figure out the story, reaching our happy ending together.

His favorite part of the game is when we say, "What happens next?" and move to the next space and lay out three cards with things on them. The current storyteller, and other storytellers when there are more people, have to pick which of the cards they think the new storyteller will choose. It's a way to remember and create a bond together knowing what the other person likes. You rank them one, two, and three. You deplete ink from your well if you don't get it correct—run out of ink and you can't finish the story and get the happy ending.

It's a great game for teaching cooperation and compromise in choosing a path together. It also exercises the adult imagination because the oldest person sets the protagonist and its relationship to their happy ending. Some of my stories have started a little rusty, but others I've honed in on a good concept for him straightaway.

I'm delighted Åsmund has taken so well to the game and continually wants to play it. It gives me a platform to teach him storytelling skills over time.

We also have the thought that we could use the format of the game, but substitute the cards for our StoryWorld card sets that we've loved making stories with for years now.

It's a tradition for Åsmund and me to have two Oreos after dinner each night. It's not a reward for eating all your dinner; it's our aperitif, if you will. We sit down with our Oreos and put on an Egyptian archeology documentary on Netflix, *The Secrets of the Saqqara Tomb*. I thought it appropriate for the Camp with its symbol of Maat logo and Åsmund's passion for all things Egyptian and archeology.

"What do you think?" I ask about fifteen minutes in.

"I love it! We need to watch this at home too."

An incredible documentary on recent ground-breaking archeological finds. We pause to resume later the next day and retreat to a hot shower.

Tonight's bedtime book is one of our newest finds: *A Year Around the Great Oak*. A lovely tale about a city boy visiting his cousin who lives on the edge of a forest. His uncle is a forester and knows all about the land and shows him a three-hundred-year-old oak tree and teaches him about all the ecology that surrounds the tree as he comes to visit once each season.

The book teaches a powerful lesson when the boy ventures into the woods at night by himself to visit the Great Oak because he's sad to leave the next day. He's trapped on a branch in the tree as wild boar are in the lake below him. He's saved by his uncle and cousin and learns it's not safe to go in the woods by himself. A perfect lesson for Åsmund to learn in the Adirondacks.

After he falls asleep, I go down to enjoy the quiet night on the balcony. I, too, experienced a lesson here at Camp Kidura about nine years ago when the lake nearly claimed my life.

It was late fall, and I was here at the Camp with my best friend from college, Jason, and my best friend from the Camp, Tim. It was a gorgeous sunny day, and the temp was in the low 60s. We thought it would be great to throw the Sunfish sailboat in the water for one last sail of the season. Tim and I had sailed dinghies and yachts before, but Jason was new to sailing.

There was a light breeze, maybe four to eight knots, perfect for him to try his hand at it. We watched him sail off and head downwind. We were having a beer on the deck of the boathouse and realized we'd not seen him for the last 5-10 minutes. Then, all of a sudden, he appeared out of breath at the boathouse.

"Where's the boat?"

"Dude, the wind picked up and all I could do was hang on. It's around the bend and tied up at a neighbor's dock."

The wind was picking up; the weather can change quickly here at times. We all jumped into the aluminum skiff with a small outboard motor, rounded a bend, and saw the Sunfish on a dock in the distance.

"I'll sail it back to the Camp guys, no worries," I said confidently, wearing a t-shirt, shorts, and life jacket. What I had failed to notice was the bank of clouds that had rolled in from the east over the mountains and the lake beginning to pick up with small waves. I had broken my own cardinal rule at the very start of this seemingly innocent voyage, a detailed look at the weather forecast.

As I sailed out from behind the shelter of the land, I was immediately hit by a big gust. I dumped the sheet, turned down, and hiked out. I quickly realized it was blowing stink out here, fifteen to eighteen knots and gusting over twenty; this was no longer a "no worries" situation. I gained some control and attempted to come up and hold a fat angle in order to get back to the Camp. It was rough going and I needed to tack to get back to

Camp; otherwise, I was going to end up across the lake on the other side.

I tacked the boat, and a wave hit the bow, popped me up a couple feet, and as I was trying to complete the tack, a gust filled the sail and capsized the boat. It was one of those action moments in life when time slows down, and you experience the whole thing like you're watching a film at 160 frames a second.

I knew it was going to be cold, but this was way colder than I expected the lake temp to be. The general rule of thumb is you have roughly five minutes in fifty-degree water until hypothermia sets in. Instead of panicking, I stayed calm and checked my watch for the time.

"I need to carefully manage my energy," I said out loud to myself, holding on to the side of the Sunfish. I got on top of the boat and was already exhausted. I debated even flipping it or just staying on top and yelling for help. The young sailor in me said go for it.

I flipped it and was in. Yes! Before I could even get my faculties together to grab the sheet and tiller, waves were pounding the side of the hull and again a puff grabbed the sail and sent me back into the water.

I didn't feel the shock of the cold this time.

I checked my watch; it had been five minutes.

I felt my energy seeping from my limbs. I looked down at my feet through the clear water; my brain was telling them to kick. They weren't moving. This was beyond bad.

I was in the middle of the lake, in a front, the waves were crashing around me and I could no longer hold on to the Sunfish. I used my remaining strength to tie the sheet around my wrist in hopes that the wind would at least push the boat to the shore. If that were the case, they'd at least find my body. I would want my family and friends to have closure.

As I leaned back in the water looking at the beautiful blue cloudy sky, a wave went over my head. I was no longer able to move or feel anything.

This is it.

At least it would be a peaceful and good death in a place I loved. I started thinking about the people I loved and closed my eyes and waited for my watery destiny to take its final hold.

Then I heard an engine in the distance. The closer it came, the deeper I drifted. Then I heard voices and forced myself to open my eyes. It was Tim and Jason in the skiff coming to my rescue. I noticed the look of panic in Tim's eyes when he got there.

"Get in, Scottie!" Jason said, reaching for me.

"He can't move at all; he's hypothermic, man. We've got to pull him in." And they did.

In the skiff, grateful to be alive, I waited in frozen agony while they flipped the Sunfish and tied it off to the back of the skiff. As they towed it back to the Camp, the wind felt like knives cutting my skin and burning my face and ears on the ride back. There was no avoiding it.

I warmed up with some blankets inside and took a warm shower after an hour. My left ear was singing with pain and pressure. On the drive back to Cleveland a couple of days later, it actually burst from the pressure with blood streaming down my neck. Come to find out a day later, I had a tear in my eardrum, and I no longer hear perfectly in that ear.

I'm ever grateful to Tim and Jason for saving my life that day, enabling me to enjoy many more trips to the Camp where I now teach these lessons to my son.

After writing all this down, I read this story to Åsmund.

He sits at attention, focused on my every word. His face contorts and he gasps when the boat goes over, eyes well up when I tie the sheet to my wrist to be found dead, sighing in relief when I'm rescued, wincing at the wind burning his Baba, crinkling his nose as blood comes out of my ear, and mouth open as I finish saying I can teach these lessons to him.

"What do you think?"

"I love it."

"What do you think the lesson is?"

"You didn't check the weather before going sailing, Baba."

"Exactly. Mother Nature is more powerful than we are. We must always respect her."

"I'm so glad we're here, together."

Me too.

CHAPTER 5

FIRESIDE STORIES

Wednesday greets us with only a peek of sun through the distant clouds behind the mountains across the lake. Our eyes take in a "good morning" from the Adirondacks, setting a humble and reflective tone for our day.

The first thing Åsmund immediately wants is to read the *Great Oak Tree* book again. I wipe the sand from my eyes, happy to oblige. We snuggle in and enjoy a second reading. Now we're ready for breakfast.

We eat breakfast together—sausages, apples, toast, cheese omelet—and the smell of thick maple bacon wafts through the cabin. That's the smell of a vacation day in our family.

Instead of writing and Legos, we decide we want to snuggle up and watch *Big Foot Family* again. There's really nothing better as a father than holding your child in your lap as you relax together. I normally wouldn't say yes to watching a movie again, but the narrative of the film is about a father using his fame to make a difference in the world and his son ultimately saving the day.

We're enveloped in warmth, enjoying ourselves snuggled up under a blanket together, the weather outside blustery and gray. These are the kind of days built for snuggle bears.

"Let's finish watching *The Saqqara Tomb*, Baba."

"Are you sure you don't want to do Legos and write?"

I know how much he prefers activities to TV, but he's adamant about remaining snuggled up in my lap and pulls the blankets up. "Alright then, but afterward, let's haul in wood from underneath the balcony and start a fire."

I load him up with three logs about his size and he makes it about halfway before losing control of them.

"I need your help, Baba. I can't do it."

"You were able to do it this far, so I know you're able to go further," I say as I struggle to keep my own large logs balanced while opening the door. "You can do it!"

He struggles valiantly and I see his own internal resolve kick in as he manages to make it to the fireplace.

"I did it!"

"I knew you could. Let's get this fire roaring." And we roar from our bellies. It feels good to roar.

The fireplace at Camp Kidura is no ordinary fireplace. It's a piece of unassuming technology that allows us to heat the entire three-story cabin. Once I have it good and hot, I add one final log, close the doors tightly, and activate the system by pushing a large iron rod in and play the choke. The house is toasty warm into the night from one good fire.

Åsmund can't wait to dive into playing "Stories of the Three Coins" again and makes me promise to play two games of stories. There's something so warm and wonderful about telling stories in front of a fire. The Danish people have a word for it: Hygge. The Danes are well known as one of the happiest cultures in the world and one of the primary reasons is their concept of Hygge—a mood of coziness and contentedness with warm ambient lighting, socks, sweaters, blankets, a crackling fire, and being together with people you care about. You can't buy Hygge; it's a feeling you can only create with others. The setting has us feeling inspired and story number eight is a good one that I'll share.

I realize that these stories we are creating give me a platform to begin and guide him along, teaching him something about life. In this story, our lone wolf, Howlie, longs to be a part of a human family because he doesn't feel a part of his own pack, because he's different. I attempt to teach Åsmund that you should not try and get what you want at the expense of others. Would our world be different if the Ponzi scheme execs had fathers that told them this story as a boy? We'll never know. The main point of the story is how the definition of family has significantly evolved, especially over the last few decades, and I want Åsmund to understand that family is who you make it.

Once upon a time, there lived a wolf. His name was Howlie.

Howlie was a good wolf, a lone wolf, and was not a carnivorous predator like his wolf pack, which liked to hunt. Howlie liked to eat berries and leaves and play amongst the trees. He became known as the "good wolf" amongst all the woodland forest animals, while his wolf pack made fun of him and belittled him for being different from them.

From a distance, Howlie would watch children and their families camping around a fire, and he wished that one day he could be around their fire too, like their dogs, but he was a wolf, and humans feared him, even though he was a good wolf that wouldn't eat little children for dinner.

How could he gain a human family's trust so that he might one day sit around a campfire eating marshmallows and drinking hot cocoa? What could he do to make that happen?

Howlie was eating some leaves for lunch by the river when he happened upon a shiny golden object stuck between some rocks. He pawed at it, wondering what it might be. All of a sudden, a genie appeared from it.

"How will I ever have a human family? I don't fit into my wolf family and I don't want to live all by myself. I see human families have such grand times together around their campfires. What can I do?"

"I cannot answer questions from you; I can only grant you three dark magic wishes."

"Lots of help you are! I need advice, not dark magic wishes."

"What if you wish for some dark things to happen to someone else, which will get you your wish?"

"As tempting as that is, I don't want to wish anything

63

bad upon anyone else in order to get what I want. That would not be right."

"But I can help you get what you want. I can help you come up with a wish."

"Genie, I don't want your dark magic; it will not help the world for me to do harm to another in order for me to get my wish. I will find another way."

Howlie wanted to just run away; however, he realized the genie could not be left to his own dark magic devices. Howlie had a good idea.

"Genie, you have to grant me my wish no matter what, as long as it uses dark magic at the expense of someone else to get what I want, right?"

"Yesssss," the genie hissed with an evil smirk on his face.

"Then I wish for you to live all of eternity in your lamp, and if ever rubbed by another being or not, you will never see the light of day again, and your magic unable to grant any wishes. I wish this wish so that I may get my wish of finding a family without your dark magic."

"Noooooo!" the genie cried out as his eyes blinked and nose twitched, his own dark magic working against him. In a great flash and puff of smoke, he disappeared back into his lamp, never to be seen again.

It worked!

Weeks later, Howlie came upon a beautiful purple

fairy who had the most wonderful smile that brightened the entire day.

"I am not afraid of you, Howlie," said the purple fairy. "I can sense you mean me no harm."

"I don't. I'm trying to find my own family that I can belong to. I don't fit into my own family because I don't like violence and killing for food, but the humans fear me, so I cannot be one of their dogs. What should I do?"

"I will help you."

"You will?"

"I will cast a shape-shifting spell on you so that you will look like a dog for fifteen minutes," said the fairy while she waved her wand. "Now run down that ridge and look for a magic mouse that will lead you to a family. Run, Howlie!"

He bounded down the ridge looking everywhere. How would he find a mouse in this forest ridge? Then, there atop a massive granite boulder, Howlie spotted a mouse with a feather on its ear, wearing rather smart clothes.

"The fairy told me I would find you here and that you will help me find a family."

"Follow me, Wolf-that-is-a-Labrador."

Howlie and the mouse ran through the forest as fast as they could and he noticed his stride was much shorter than when he was a wolf.

They reached a clearing and saw a mom, dad, son, and

their family dog sitting around a fire laughing and camping together.

"Go now, young wolf." said the mouse, in a rather stoic way, as if he was about to witness a prophecy come true.

Howlie ran across the field to the family dog to make friends, but the dog could sense he was no ordinary dog and barked because he seemed bigger than he looked. He greeted the son, who was five years old.

"Where did you come from, boy? Where's your home?" asked the son.

Howlie gave him a big wet kiss, wagging his tail. He liked the boy very much. The mom and dad petted Howlie too.

This family is perfect, Howlie thought to himself. He went behind the tent and picked a wildflower and brought it over to the mom.

"Thanks, boy! You're such a good dog. Where's your home?"

Howlie whimpered, resting his head in her lap. He knew his fifteen minutes were running out.

"Mommy, can we keep him?"

"Of course we can."

And just then, the spell took hold of Howlie. His paws tingled and every hair vibrated for a fraction of a second. He felt different. He was a dog.

He started running on his new legs as fast as he could and ran into the forest.

"I forgot to tell you the spell would be permanent if you joined the family," the fairy said as she zipped in front of Howlie, stopping him in his tracks. "Go back to your new family now. You are the legend that has been foretold, the wolf who became a dog, and must fulfill your destiny."

Howlie came barreling out of the woods, jumping on the son and kissing his face. The two rolled around together playing in a large field of grass as the sun glowed red and orange after just having dipped below the horizon.

"Son, time for bed, honey, we're getting up early to leave," said the dad.

"But we have to stay just a little longer!" cried the mom and son.

Howlie was excited to have his dream come true, but didn't want to leave the forest and all his friends. Then he remembered an old cave where miners used to live. He had seen shiny stones in it. He knew the son and dad would like them. Humans always loved finding them and would leap up in joy.

"Bark! Bark!" He ran off and the boy followed closely behind.

They ran through the forest together as fast as they could.

When they reached the cave, the boy did not want to go in. Howlie could see that he was scared. He went in and retrieved one of the clear rocks and brought it to the boy.

"Diamonds!" the boy shouted. "Let's go show Dad. Now we can stay here for sure!"

"Bark!" Howlie reached the dad before the boy, his tail wagging as fast as a hummingbird's wings.

"Dad, Howlie found a diamond; now we can stay!"

The dad and mom looked closely at the stone, both mouths wide open.

"I knew you were something special," said the mom.

"We're going to build a cabin and live right here, as a family," said the dad, tears of joy welling up in his eyes as he wrapped his arms around his boy and Howlie.

"We'll call you Diamond," said the boy.

And so it came to be that Howlie got his wish and his story became known as the Diamond Legend to forest creatures and humans alike. He had a family, a new name, and the dad built the most beautiful wood cabin right where they had met. Howlie lived in that cabin with his new family, and he and the boy would play in the forest with all his wild friends that he loved so much.

And they all lived happily ever after.

"That one was great, Baba! I love how light magic wins."

Our story now finished, Åsmund looks tired and pinches his index finger and thumb together while squinting his eyes and says with a smirk, "How about a little snack?" Snack time of Doritos and juice leads right into a nice little fireside nap together for thirty minutes. When we wake up, we look outside and see a front rolling in. The sky turns into an organism of fine mist with tiny drops of rain falling intermittently as if the Camp has conferred with Mother Nature and is prompting us to press on with our Lego and writing endeavors.

"I think it's going to be a good day for us to stay in and start building Lego Skull Island and for me to write chapter three. Sound good, buddy?"

"Yeah, I think so."

We get to work on our projects at the table and we're having a great time, both of us making significant progress.

The song "A Little More" by Eric Hutchinson comes on, and Åsmund stops, closes his eyes, and starts swaying his head like he did to the song "Way Back When." It's so amazing to see this little person get lost in a song he's never heard, to see its melodies, harmonies, and rhythm take his mind somewhere else. I know that feeling. "Sibelius Valse Triste" still has an other-worldly effect on me. In fact, science says people that get goosebumps from music have brains that are wired differently (Clay, J. (2017). If you get the chills from music, you may

69

have a unique brain. *USC News*. Retrieved from: https://neurosciencenews.com/music-chills-neuroscience-6167/).

I'm elated after I finish writing the chapter. I read a few sentences to Åsmund and he announces that it's time for a break playing hyper bouncy ball. The "Moon Ball" is pretty incredible. A bouncy ball is one of the great toys of childhood; its simplicity and approachability makes for great fun. We're going to go back to the Imagination Station tomorrow so we can get a yoyo for just this reason.

We go outside for our break and discover the ice in front of the balcony has receded out to the lake.

"I can't believe it, Baba. Look, the ice is moving!" We're literally watching nature at work, slowly over time. Camp Kidura makes observing nature so accessible; we're situated amongst it. Even in the game room inside the boathouse, we're literally on the water looking across the lake at a sea of pine trees forming the undulating shoreline. Some spirited games of foosball and shuffleboard entertain us for an hour, and we decide it's noodle soup time.

After winding down with soups and a bedtime shower, it's finally book time. That's basically prime-time for Åsmund and me each and every day, whether we're at the Camp or not, and the main event tonight is *The Wisdom of Trees*.

We learn all about how trees can communicate with each other through the fungal network on their roots and how they distribute resources as a community in order to grow and remain healthy together. A nice parable to life as humans. I'm a big fan of biomimicry as it relates to not only product engineering but also societal and community constructs. The models within nature have been tested over and over throughout time and have evolved to work well in their design not only for specific organisms and animals, but as it relates to the whole.

Like the network of trees, my connection with Åsmund is helping us both grow, compounding upon itself every day we spend time here together.

"Do you hear that?" he murmurs, eyes half mast.

"I do."

We hear the lake gently lapping against the shore, its rhythm in step with our heartbeats.

I've got goosebumps.

We drift asleep soundly, together.

CHAPTER 6

YO-YO, MICROCLIMATE

Our day begins slowly with sunny snuggles, the rays illuminating our room covering us in a blanket of warmth. I'm excited to see the sun after yesterday being so dreary. In life, it takes the lows in order to set context to the highs. Sometimes it feels like Camp Kidura intrinsically knows how to create a balanced dichotomy for our stay. When every day brings sunshine, you're not able to appreciate it as much without the gray days—you need both.

"Good morning, boys!" Tina cheerfully says when I answer the Facetime call.

"G' morning, Mommy!" Åsmund shouts in the background.

"Hi, Åsmund! How are you?" says Colby, our six-year-old next-door neighbor who's friends with Åsmund. She's over visiting Tina and is excited to see Åsmund and asks him for a tour of the Camp. He is delighted to show her around the cabin and they spend the next thirty minutes on the phone. Åsmund is a very social person and enjoys spending time with his friends playing. I'm happy he gets to see her; it gives us a little balance and time apart, if only for a half an hour. I drink a cup of my favorite cold brew coffee quietly on the balcony.

After breakfast, we open the day with a game of "Stories of the Three Coins," but this time, we use the StoryWorld set of cards entitled "Tales from the Sea." The illustrations are so detailed, and we've been using them for years now. It makes for a fun little story.

After an outdoor Flying Sabuki climbing break, it's off to work on our foosball and shuffleboard skills yet again. Important stuff, indeed.

The temperature is in the low sixties and we play about fifteen games of Uno on the balcony in the sunlight.

Then it's back to building Legos and writing the book. I'm feeling really good about the progress we've both made over the course of the week.

We've stuck to our goals and inspired each other to keep at it. There have been times I've not felt like writing and Åsmund has said, "Remember, it's important to finish the book, Baba. Keep working on it." His ability to really listen when we talk about things that are important to each other continues to impress me. I pay attention to his aspirations closely as well.

Time for an Oreo break on the deck. "I've got an idea, Baba. Let's make shadow puppets on the deck. The sun is at a perfect angle where we're sitting." I forgot how fun it is to take a moment to figure out different shapes with your hands and having happy accidents that turn into an animal you had never even intended to make. We make so many: bugs, octopus, squid, moose, raven, ghost, monster, tee pee, and eagles, as well as at least five different species of bird. He makes one of the coolest-looking ghosts before we get ready to head to Lake Placid.

"I can't wait to get a yoyo, Baba! What else are we going to get?" he chirps from his car seat.

"We're going to pick out something nice for Mommy and Miss Sarah."

"Nothing more for me?"

"No, just the yo-yo."

"Okay, we'll find Mommy something she'll like."

I'm continually trying to balance his sense of consumerism and entitlement with wanting to enrich his life with experiences and toys that promote his cognitive development. I also don't want him to become obsessed with money at too young of an age, or any age for that matter. There are all of these little nuances to being a parent that no one tells you about before becoming one. It's an amalgamation of all the little daily interactions that add up to the result.

He picks out a light-up Duncan yo-yo, very similar to the green and orange one I had as a child. I loved my yo-yo when I was his age. It was so much to learn how to walk the dog and cradle it. I spot a really cool sweatshirt with a mountain and bear designed with negative space and colorful geometric shapes.

"Think Mommy will like this?"

"Mommy will love it!"

Done and done. Imagination Station always delivers with a smile.

We walk down the street. Our next stop is the Christmas Shoppe. Unfortunately, it's closed today. We normally visit the owner Scott and his mom to buy some Christmas ornaments for the tree with our names written on them. It's a nice tradition we have to think of Christmas no matter what time of year we're up here. We'll see him next time.

We saunter down the entire main street, laughing and playing, to the last building, a restaurant called "Players." I adore the place for its wings and great view of Mirror Lake. Åsmund is quick to show the owner his new yo-yo that lights up.

"That's a wonderful toy you have. Did you just get that?"

"It's not a toy, it's a yo-yo, and yes, at Imagination Station."

The owner and I share a hearty laugh at his candid answer, correcting him that it's not a toy, but a proper yo-yo. We enjoy a quiet lunch and have a chat with Tina on the phone.

There are numerous Flying Sabuki sightings on the way home and I'm taken even deeper into their culture through Åsmund's vivid imagination. Apparently, Flying Sabuki can sense if a kid can be trusted, and if so, they will reveal themselves.

"Baba, if you try to hide really well at the Camp, I'll see if I can get one [Flying Sabuki] to come out."

He takes a little nap on the ride home and is refreshed and ready to play games.

"Can I have some Scooby Snacks?"

"Sure can."

I've rarely said no to a request for Scooby Snacks on vacation. He and I both love Scooby Doo. We watch all of the old and new cartoon episodes and movies together. He was Scooby Doo on his third Halloween. He respects the Scooby Snacks. I'm careful never to use them as a reward for anything. When he asks for them, I usually ask him how many he has had today, and why does he think it's a good time to have them. But on vacation, unless it's nighttime: Let's have some Scooby Snacks!

We pair our chewy, fruity treats with a game of Battleship on the balcony. Such a classic game that he has an incredible ability to beat me at—every time. I love that Battleship has taught him coordinates. We played it one Saturday at the yacht club after finishing our work hours cleaning windows that day with many nostalgic looks from the old salty dogs that are my new friends.

We joined a non-profit yacht club this past year, Northeast Yacht Club, where we keep *Escapade*. We talk about how we plan to play Battleship and build Legos on *Escapade* this summer and have campouts on the boat.

"Let's take a hike, Baba."

"I'd love to, Åsmund." It's the most beautiful and warm day we've had yet. We walk up the steps and notice all the snow has melted from them. The dirt road that was frozen yesterday is now mud.

"Look, Baba! That puddle isn't like frozen glass ice anymore. It's water!"

He's an observant little guy. He had so much fun smashing the ice from this puddle the other day and our hike is about to get even better.

"Do you hear that, Åsmund? Stop, listen."

We both focus our hearing.

"I hear lots of water." he says in a hushed tone.

We run up the road and see the stream that was once frozen now raging with water pouring under the small land bridge we're standing on.

"Can you believe we're seeing winter change to spring right in front of our eyes?"

"Look at all of this water!" His eyes are wide, mouth agape. He's so excited to witness what he had just seen the day before as frozen, now a surging torrent of melt water.

As we walk down by the lake, we suddenly feel warm.

"Why is it so warm?" he asks me as we continue walking toward the lake, now tucked behind some trees.

"Look up there." I point up to the clearing and the open snow.

"I'll bet if we walk over this way, it will get really cold," I say as we continue our walk.

"Whoa! It's so cold, Baba! You were right!" A brisk wind picks up, delivering a fresh wafting of cold air off the remaining snow in the open clearing, and it feels about twenty degrees cooler. We walk back and forth twenty yards north to south a handful of times experiencing the microclimate phenomenon.

We hike back to the camp and have a nice chat with Tina. She's so excited to hear about our little microclimate adventure and misses us.

As per usual, it's ramen noodle soup for Åsmund and another serving of the Kidura Casserole while we watch an episode of *Ancient Aliens*. Åsmund is fascinated by extraterrestrial anything.

We finish our day with a bowl of ice cream together over about ten games of "Kaleva." The game has character cards from the ancient epic tale of the Finnish people, *The Kalevela*. That mythology of the Kalevela was passed down for generations as tone poems until Elias Lönnrot published them into a book between 1835 and 1849. The game is inspired by the stories with a beautifully illustrated game board and cards, and play is simple with randomness driving strategy and games lasting five minutes or so.

The characters' names are uniquely Finnish, like Ukko, Terna, Ahti, and Kulervo, and it's fun to expose Åsmund to my family's heritage and language while we play. Åsmund loves how other languages sound and is always keen to learn new words. In one of his school projects, his answer to "How do I want to give back to the world?" was "To learn many languages."

I wonder if he'll work for the UN one day like my mom's sister Helena did. She perished in a car accident driving to see me when I was born. I believe her to be my guardian angel of sorts because I have escaped death numerous times in my life by what seems to be happenstance, but I've felt some kind of... the best way of explaining it to be "a guiding force" protecting me during those times. We have yet to fully understand or study consciousness, so for now, I choose to believe Helena continues to watch over me for her little sister.

Book time is our Camp hit *Snow Friends* again and we snuggle in for a good night's sleep before our final day.

CHAPTER 7

WILD CENTER

A white foggy haze grips the sky outside of our window this morning. It's as if the Camp asked Mother Nature to give us a final day to remember and an opaque filter over our beautiful morning mountain range says, "Stay in bed and snuggle on this last morning at the Camp." We contentedly oblige and delight in the warmth of the poofy down comforter. The temperature is especially crisp this morning.

I'm always a little sad when I wake up on the last morning here at Camp Kidura. My only comfort is that I know I'll come back because I love it so much. Being here at the Camp for a week with only Åsmund has changed me as a man and a father—I've been enlightened with a deeper understanding of his persona. I've touched wisdom and felt the symbiotic father and son connection that only uninterrupted time together can reveal.

Åsmund takes down a maple sausage in record time and immediately re-engages construction of Lego Skull Island. I make my last two eggs into a cheese omelet with ham and mentally prepare myself for all the dad things I need to do in order to depart for Cleveland promptly at 7 am tomorrow.

The fog begins to clear, revealing the forest across the lake, sweeping itself off its own feet as if in a waltz with the icy frozen lake.

"Quick, let's take a picture of all this, Baba!" We run out on the balcony, cameras in hand, and immediately take note of the distinct smell the rainfall and meltwater activated last night. We both deeply inhale, and the cold air enlightens our spirits through our olfactory sense. I smell moss, pine, mud, and moisture that's reminiscent of a bottled air freshener, but oh so much better—so captivating.

We take our pics, but for me, it just never seems to capture the moment as it felt. I wish I could capture all of the experience: humidity, temperature, wind, smells—everything. I find pictures, smells, and particularly music are helpful triggers to bring me back in time to this moment later in life. I want to travel back to this time whenever I want, for a Flying Sabuki to open a portal to these precious days.

We get dressed for the weather and head out to our grand finale for the week at the Wild Center in Tupper Lake, NY. It's the natural history museum of the Adirondacks and we've both been so excited for it ever since we bought the tickets on Tuesday.

There have been thunderstorms and high wind warnings for today and I call ahead to make sure it will be open for us. Åsmund and I aren't afraid of a little weather, but dangerous weather warnings are another thing. I take heed and have learned my lessons to not misjudge or discount the power and fury that nature has over humanity. However, our family always says, there's no bad weather, only bad clothing choices. We garrulously protest when others present miniscule reasons, such as cold, for not enjoying a gorgeous walk in the snow.

We're greeted at the Wild Center by a wonderful woman in the car park booth who takes our names and engages with Åsmund in a way only a mother that loves being a mother can. He's even more excited because the first thing we're going to do is visit the otters!

I happened to see an otter in the wild in front of the balcony a couple days ago. He was very small compared to the otters at the Wild Center. He popped up out of the water and ran across the ice, diving into the underbrush and disappearing from sight immediately. Åsmund was so upset he didn't see him that day, and is now elated to be able to see these two otters swimming and rolling around in the water together. *My goodness are they happy creatures,* I think to myself watching them flip and turn.

Then it was off to explore the great tree and rope bridge canopy tour. The wayfinding of the park is striking in its design. We've seen our fair share of nature centers and this is cool. Giant conical cap structures sit atop multiple large steel tubes in a tee-pee-like layout, greeting us along our walk across the canopy and to the sights and experiences.

Our first stop is the rope bridge that leads to the great tree. The woman at the car park said to make sure we go down to the very bottom for a surprise. After crossing the bridge and entering the tree, the smell of Christmas tree pine takes over our noses. It is actually pungent, though certainly not offensive. It's like a blast of Christmas spirit from Santa himself.

At the bottom of the steps inside the tree are mama and cub black bears sleeping by a soft light on a lush and thick bed of freshly cut pine branches. Little windows in the tree beckon us to peer inside and therein are deeper learnings and facts about the life of a tree and all that surrounds it. I could've spent hours reading each and every one, but Åsmund wants to explore all the bridges.

The twenty-foot-wide cable and rope spider's nest immediately calls Åsmund onto it. Such an experience being on this web two stories off the ground. We head up to the eagle's nest, a structure enveloped in branches to look like a larger-than-life real nest. The view here is spectacular and you can see the Adirondacks for miles and miles. There are tubes with the mountain name on them that we peer through that highlight the various high peaks, and we have to try them all out.

We go back to the trail that points to the river and begin ascending down, weighing each step carefully on the frozen ice that occupies the middle of the trail. We point out interesting things we both see, and work together finding a safe trail down to the Raclette River. There's a deck lookout and we stop to observe the tree tannins that color its waters a tan hue. One of those rare times I remember to take a selfie.

I didn't grow up taking pictures of myself, being a "xennial." That's the gap generation between X and Millennial from the late 70s to early 80s. We're unique in that we remember life distinctly before the information age, the internet, and smart mobile devices, yet grew up with the technology that has become so pervasive across our society. Probably why I like typewriters and vinyl; the tactile experience is nostalgic for me. I truly appreciate "analog" and "digital." They both bring great things to life when kept in balance.

All of my annual trips up to Camp Kidura are about just that: balance. This trip in particular has been about bonding together as a father and son, without distractions, and creating our own presence together. I check my screen time metric and have rarely used my phone for anything other than to take a photo of something we're doing or to add a note to Dabble Writer for writing on this book. My focus has been observing, remembering, and feeling the innocent moments with my son that make life so grand.

While Åsmund may or may not remember all the things about our vacation trip to the Wild Center, I know I will. I have a mental mode that I'm able to turn on when I'm presently interested in something and just remember all of it. Today was one of those days.

The grand highlight of the Wild Center for us is when we meet Cora the Raven. One of the naturalists, Shannon, tells us all about how she was hurt and would never fly again, but loves jumping from branch to branch and is so social that she can even say "hello." We learn how amazingly talented and intelligent ravens are and how they can mimic thousands of sounds. She is so active and really engaging with us.

We are both astounded when Shannon tells us the peregrine falcon can dive and hit speeds over 200mph, the fastest hunting bird in the skies. This particular bird had been a working hunting bird and is now here at the nature center for retirement at thirteen years of age.

We head to Tupper Lake for lunch and go into "Well Dressed Food," where we are greeted by giant TV screen menus, glass cases, and a hipster-looking mountain woman preparing to-go boxes en masse.

"Pickup?" she says while fastidiously working.

"No, dine in for two, please."

"So you know, it's going to be at least thirty minutes for me to get to you."

And at that, we leave. Across the street, I see "The Swiss Kitchen," which did not pop up on

Google Maps for restaurants. This is the difference of generations at work here. The analog to the digital.

The Swiss Kitchen has a red roof, vintage type-face logo, and the feeling that generations of citizens come here not just for the delicious home-style meals, but also for the conversation and community. Every square inch of the inside walls is covered edge to edge with picture frames of people through the decades. One row of booths lines the left wall and there's a counter to the right. This is our spot.

Our waitress, around the same age as the one across the street, greets us warmly, setting the tone for what will become my favorite meal of the entire vacation.

"How are you guys today?" her eyes say kindly from behind retro cool frames and her COVID required mask. COVID has really forced me to look into people's eyes, because my primary cue until now had always been their smile.

"Good." This is Åsmund's default descriptor for just about anything.

Åsmund orders one chocolate chip pancake with orange juice and I ask her what the locals all love to eat. "That's easy. Patty melt or turkey dinner, definitely some poutine with curds."

"Patty melt and poutine with curds it is! Thank you so much."

Åsmund waits patiently for our food to arrive. He's such a good boy. I read one of the local free magazine's story about a British massacre in Vermont in 1788 and how its tale was almost lost if not for one book written that gathered all the local history on the event into one document. Makes me think about how one book can change people's lives or recant a piece of history that would have otherwise been lost. There are so many examples of this in history.

For this book, I'm hoping it inspires other parents to take a week without digital distractions to connect with their child, or one of their children. I love the family vacation, but there is something so intimate about a parent and child coexisting together in a nature-based setting for an entire week and profoundly getting to know another person's rhythms and pulse. I'm so glad we did this spring break vacation at Camp Kidura and am even more glad that I wrote a novella about it—my first book.

If I lived up here, I'd eat that poutine at least once a week. The gravy is so hearty and clearly homemade. When asked how it tastes by the waitress and construction guys at the bar, I say, "Put that gravy in a sports bottle. I'd gain seventy pounds eating this poutine every day if I lived up here."

They all laugh.

Upon our return home, Åsmund and I enjoy a glorious two-and-a-half-hour nap together. We both could barely keep awake on our drive home and played rock, paper, scissors to pass the last ten minutes of the drive.

Åsmund finishes Lego Skull Island while I write this last chapter. He has so much fun playing with the characters on the island and pretending they were pirates using their map in search of treasure, that I think he has lost his stamina for finishing the project.

"Are you going to finish the island soon?"

"Yeah," he mutters, deep in play as one of the pirates splashes into the water.

"My fingers are getting tired and running out of energy. Do you think I should just stop or finish writing the book?"

"You have to finish it, Baba. It's important," he says with a little shock to his voice that I would even consider quitting.

"Do you think you can finish Skull Island while I finish writing? We can finish together."

"I do." He puts down the characters with

purpose adjacent to his work area to undoubtedly watch him finish. His focus comes back as he picks up the instruction book.

He cracks a smile and raises his hand in the air, holding up his index finger as he announces what step he is about to embark upon. He is excited to finish his Lego build this time and peers at the treasure inside Skull Island.

My life treasure was found when this little guy was born, my head and heart say speaking in tandem.

I have the last of my Kidura Casserole and Åsmund has noodle soup for dinner followed by the last bit of ice cream. We watched the last of *Big Foot Family* while eating and I packed up all the toys, games, and Legos.

"So what did you think of our vacation here?" I ask after we finished reading *Snow Friends* and the *Great Oak* book in bed.

"Good. I think we should come here once a year together."

"I think that's a great idea, Åsmund. We'll do that."

CHAPTER 8

BYE, CAMP KIDURA

The Adirondacks seem to have plotted on our final night to give us a morning to remember. I can see a little of my breath while opening my eyes. The color of the room is crisp with a white glow from the window. We awake not to sun or rain, but snow. Beautiful baby flakes create a white blanket on top of every last tree branch and the lake is the stage for the wind to put on its play, *A Magic Flurry*, with multiple cyclonic characters and twists of flurries whipping across the stage, expertly choreographed by Mother Nature.

I got up at 3 am to finish writing the last chapter of the book. There was no way I was going to let myself forget some of the details of yesterday.

I needed to prove to myself, and to Åsmund, that I could finish a book in a week. My fatherly mission of a meaningful week with my son was accomplished, and with great success. This was at the top of the thriving scale. I consciously worked hard to forget the mental restraints of adult life in order to be open to the possibilities and active imagination that only my five-year-old son could evince from me. To have written this book, quite possibly the most important thing I've done to date, is the souvenir from this trip for me.

We both take note of the crisp winter air and how beautiful the blanket of snow is that has covered everything in sight. The car is packed with our belongings and we begin our drive up the dirt road, now frozen again, as it had been when we came.

"Bye, Camp Kidura!" I say, waving in the rearview mirror.

"Bye, Camp Kidura, we'll miss you. See you next year!" Åsmund bellows in an innocent and sincere voice. "I can sense the Camp saying goodbye, Baba. I sense it."

"Yes, the three of us have bonded, haven't we?" I say, intentionally personifying the Camp itself. We've done this many times over the course of the week, and right now, it feels more than real.

"Yeah, we have. The Camp misses us already. I feel it."

"Me too, buddy."

"Do you think the Camp is a he or a she, Baba?"

"I think it's a spirit, son, not male or female, but omnipotent." I take a mental note to explain animism to him another year.

"Yeah, omnipotent." He enunciates the word as best he can, his confident and adorable voice letting me know he just learned what that word meant. I look forward to hearing him pull that word out around someone else.

We pull onto Panther Mountain Road and head west toward home.

"Look at that Flying Sabuki; it's a queen! All the Flying Sabuki are going to miss us too, Baba."

"I know they will."

But I know we will revisit them and our moments here in the pages of my book—and in our wonderful imaginations, together.

ABOUT THE AUTHOR

E.S. Curry is an insatiable renaissance man that lives in Cleveland, OH with his wife Tina, son Åsmund, and dogs Saoirse and Santtu. He designs brand strategies and marketing campaigns, loves writing outside the datastream on a Royal typewriter while listening to classical music on vinyl, playing piano and guitar, racing his sailing yacht *Escapade*, and imagining bedtime stories with his son. For over 20 years, he's worked with iconic brands around the world, including Arnold Palmer, Olympics, Fashion Week, and numerous non-profit initiatives. This is his first book. Learn more at escurry.com.

ABOUT THE FLYING SABUKI

Do you know what a "Flying Sabuki" is?

During a week's vacation together in the Adirondack Mountains, writer E.S. Curry discovers, through nature and his son Åsmund's imagination, what this phenomenon is and so much more. This uplifting testament to the joys of fatherhood is a must-read for anyone who wants to learn about the connection and bonding rituals that cement the father-son relationship—electronics and distraction free.

E.S. Curry and his son Åsmund teach us about working together for mutual success, the Danish concept of Hygge, driving character and values through storytelling, and how being amongst nature creates an environment for connectedness. While there are scores of books for expecting fathers, *The*

Flying Sabuki opens an intimate window into the formative Kindergarten years of a father and son relationship with a positive foundation.

The Flying Sabuki is a heartwarming tale that's the perfect holiday or Father's Day gift and a great book for parents looking for real-world insights on bonding with their child.

Made in United States
Orlando, FL
07 January 2022

13048191R00067